GOD'S LITTLE INSTRUCTION BOOK

FOR THE CLASS OF 2008

GOD'S LITTLE INSTRUCTION BOOK
FOR THE CLASS OF 2008

HONOR **HB** BOOKS

FROM DAVID C. COOK

GOD'S LITTLE INSTRUCTION BOOK FOR THE CLASS OF 2008
Published by Honor Books®, an imprint of
David C. Cook
4050 Lee Vance View
Colorado Springs, CO 80918 U.S.A.

David C. Cook Distribution Canada
55 Woodslee Avenue, Paris, Ontario, Canada N3L 3E5

David C. Cook U.K., Kingsway Communications
Eastbourne, East Sussex BN23 6NT, England

David C. Cook and the graphic circle C logo
are registered trademarks of Cook Communications Ministries.

ISBN 978-1-56292-947-3

© 2008 Honor Books

The Team: Ingrid Beck, Melanie Larson, Jaci Schneider
Interior Design: Karen Athen
Cover Design: studiogearbox.com
Cover Photo: Steve Gardner/Pixelworks Studio

Printed in the United States of America
First Edition 2008

1 2 3 4 5 6 7 8 9 10

121807

INTRODUCTION

Congratulations! As a member of the Class of 2008, you have the privilege and responsibility of being part of the most important group of people on earth—those who will be setting the pace, establishing the values, and initiating the changes for a world that suddenly finds itself face to face with the future.

Like every generation that has come before, you will encounter enormous challenges as well as amazing opportunities. And you are bound to find that you will be confronted with difficult questions and complex issues for which there are no precedents. You will truly be going where no one has gone before—except God! How will you find the answers you need?

In *God's Little Instruction Book for the Class of 2008*, we at Honor Books offer you God's timeless wisdom taken from the one book that will never be obsolete—the Bible. We hope the truths presented in these pages will serve as cherished resources for you as you launch out into the depths of human possibility and potential.

FOR THE CLASS OF 2008

The future belongs to those who believe
in the beauty of their dreams.
—ELEANOR ROOSEVELT

**May he give you the desire of your
heart and make all your plans succeed.**
Psalm 20:4

FOR THE CLASS OF 2008

To accomplish great things we must not only act,
but also dream; not only plan, but also believe.
—ANATOLE FRANCE

**For Christ is the end of the law for
righteousness to everyone who
believes.**

Romans 10:4 NKJV

FOR THE CLASS OF 2008

The journey of a thousand miles
begins with one step.
—LAO-TZU

**For God did not give us a spirit of
timidity, but a spirit of power, of love
and of self-discipline.**

2 Timothy 1:7

FOR THE CLASS OF 2008

Laughter gives us distance. It allows
us to step back from an event, deal
with it, and then move on.
—BOB NEWHART

**For our light affliction, which is but for
a moment, is working for us a far more
exceeding and eternal weight of glory.**
2 Corinthians 4:17 NKJV

FOR THE CLASS OF 2008

God is the God of promise. He keeps his word, even when that seems impossible, even when the circumstances seem to point to the opposite.
—COLIN URQUHART

What I have said, that will I bring about; what I have planned, that will I do.

Isaiah 46:11

FOR THE CLASS OF 2008

But it was not by dialectic that it pleased God to save His people; "for the kingdom of God consisteth in simplicity of faith, not in wordy contention."

—St. Ambrose

If you do not stand firm in your faith, you will not stand at all.

Isaiah 7:9

FOR THE CLASS OF 2008

Believe in yourself! Have faith in your abilities!
Without a humble but reasonable confidence in your
own powers you cannot be successful or happy.

—NORMAN VINCENT PEALE

**There's nothing better than being wise,
Knowing how to interpret the meaning
of life.**

**Wisdom puts light in the eyes,
And gives gentleness to words and
manners.**

Ecclesiastes 8:1 MSG

FOR THE CLASS OF 2008

When I look back on all these worries, I remember the story of the old man who said on his deathbed that he had had a lot of trouble in his life, most of which had never happened.

—WINSTON CHURCHILL

Do not worry about your life, what you will eat or drink; or about your body, what you will wear.

Matthew 6:25

FOR THE CLASS OF 2008

GOD'S LITTLE INSTRUCTION BOOK

Sin is not hurtful because it is forbidden, but it is forbidden because it is hurtful.

—Benjamin Franklin

I am troubled by my sin.

Psalm 38:18

FOR THE CLASS OF 2008

We must accept finite disappointment,
but never lose infinite hope.
—MARTIN LUTHER KING JR.

**Though he slay me, yet I will hope in
him.**

Job 13:15

FOR THE CLASS OF 2008

The only way to discover the limits of the possible is to go beyond them into the impossible.

—ARTHUR C. CLARKE

Jesus said to him, "If you can believe, all things are possible to him who believes."

Mark 9:23 NKJV

FOR THE CLASS OF 2008

We are all faced with a series of great opportunities brilliantly disguised as impossible situations.
—CHARLES R. SWINDOLL

Fight the good fight of the faith. Take hold of the eternal life to which you were called when you made your good confession in the presence of many witnesses.

1 Timothy 6:12

FOR THE CLASS OF 2008

Wisdom is not a product of schooling but of the lifelong attempt to acquire it.
—ALBERT EINSTEIN

Wisdom and truth will enter the very center of your being, filling your life with joy.

Proverbs 2:10 TLB

FOR THE CLASS OF 2008

Speak when you are angry—and you'll make the best speech you'll ever regret.
—LAURENCE J. PETER

Watch your words and hold your tongue; you'll save yourself a lot of grief.

Proverbs 21:23 MSG

FOR THE CLASS OF 2008

Never, for fear of feeble man, restrain your witness.
—CHARLES SPURGEON

If anyone publicly acknowledges me as his friend, I will openly acknowledge him as my friend before my father in heaven.

Matthew 10:32 TLB

FOR THE CLASS OF 2008

When the character of a man is not
clear to you, look at his friends.
—JAPANESE PROVERB

**A righteous man is cautious in
friendship.**

Proverbs 12:26

FOR THE CLASS OF 2008

GOD'S LITTLE INSTRUCTION BOOK

We need to pay more attention to how we treat
people than to how they treat us.
—JOYCE MEYERS

**You must love others as much as
yourself.**

Mark 12:31 TLB

FOR THE CLASS OF 2008

Bad times have a scientific value. These are occasions a good learner would not miss.
—RALPH WALDO EMERSON

Blessed is the man who perseveres under trial, because when he has stood the test, he will receive the crown of life that God has promised to those who love him.

James 1:12

FOR THE CLASS OF 2008

Things are not always what they seem.
—PHAEDRUS

The LORD does not look at the things man looks at. Man looks at the outward appearance, but the LORD looks at the heart.

1 Samuel 16:7

FOR THE CLASS OF 2008

Death is more universal than life;
everyone dies; not everyone lives.
—A. SACHS

**I have come that they may have life,
and have it to the full.**

John 10:10

FOR THE CLASS OF 2008

Wise men talk because they have something to say;
fools, because they have to say something.
—PLATO

**The mouth of the righteous man utters
wisdom, and his tongue speaks what is
just.**

Psalm 37:30

FOR THE CLASS OF 2008

The remarkable thing about fearing God is that when you fear God you fear nothing else, whereas if you do not fear God you fear everything else.

—OSWALD CHAMBERS

God is our refuge and strength, an ever-present help in trouble. Therefore we will not fear.

Psalm 46:1-2

FOR THE CLASS OF 2008

Where I found truth, there found I my
God, who is the truth itself.
—St. Augustine

Seek first his kingdom and his righteousness, and all these things will be given to you as well.

Matthew 6:33

FOR THE CLASS OF 2008

Only a sweet and virtuous soul,
like seasoned timber, never gives.
—GEORGE HERBERT

**Let your eyes look straight ahead, fix
your gaze directly before you.**

Proverbs 4:25

FOR THE CLASS OF 2008

Courage is fear that has said its prayers.
—DOROTHY BERNARD

But Christ is faithful as a son over God's house. And we are his house, if we hold on to our courage and the hope of which we boast.

Hebrews 3:6

FOR THE CLASS OF 2008

Willpower does not change men. Time does
not change men. Christ does.
—HENRY DRUMMOND

**Now to him who is able to do
immeasurably more than all we ask or
imagine, according to his power that is
at work within us.**

Ephesians 3:20

FOR THE CLASS OF 2008

The only way to learn strong faith
is to endure great trials.
—GEORGE MÜLLER

**My dear brothers, stand firm. Let
nothing move you. Always give
yourselves fully to the work of the
Lord, because you know that your labor
in the Lord is not in vain.**

1 Corinthians 15:58

FOR THE CLASS OF 2008

To have a right to do a thing is not at all the same as to be right in doing it.
—G. K. CHESTERTON

This is what the LORD says: "Stand at the crossroads and look; ask for the ancient paths, ask where the good way is, and walk in it, and you will find rest for your souls."

Jeremiah 6:16

FOR THE CLASS OF 2008

Effort only fully releases its reward
after a person refuses to quit.
—NAPOLEON HILL

Don't quit in hard times; pray all the harder.

Romans 12:12 MSG

FOR THE CLASS OF 2008

I try to avoid looking forward or backward,
and try to keep looking upward.
—CHARLOTTE BRONTË

**I have set the LORD always before me.
Because he is at my right hand, I will
not be shaken.**

Psalm 16:8

FOR THE CLASS OF 2008

All works of love are works of peace.
—MOTHER TERESA

I have told you these things, so that in me you may have peace. In this world you will have trouble. But take heart! I have overcome the world.

John 16:33

FOR THE CLASS OF 2008

When we long for life without difficulties, remind us that oaks grow strong in contrary winds and diamonds are made under pressure.

—PETER MARSHALL

Perseverance must finish its work so that you may be mature and complete, not lacking anything.

James 1:4

FOR THE CLASS OF 2008

Be courteous to all, but intimate with few,
and let those few be well tried before you
give them your confidence.
—GEORGE WASHINGTON

**He who walks with wise men will be
wise.**

Proverbs 13:20 NKJV

FOR THE CLASS OF 2008

God will not demand more from you than you can do. Whatever God asks of you, he will give you the strength to do.
—ERWIN W. LUTZER

So now, go. I am sending you to Pharaoh to bring my people the Israelites out of Egypt.

Exodus 3:10

FOR THE CLASS OF 2008

Have courage for the great sorrows of life and
patience for the small ones; and when you have
laboriously accomplished your daily task,
go to sleep in peace. God is awake.
—VICTOR HUGO

**He will not let your foot slip—he who
watches over you will not slumber.**

Psalm 121:3

FOR THE CLASS OF 2008

Five great enemies to peace inhabit with us: greed, ambition, envy, anger, and pride.
—PETRARCH

The LORD blesses his people with peace.

Psalm 29:11

FOR THE CLASS OF 2008

Since He looked upon me, my heart is not my
own. He hath run away to heaven with it.
—SAMUEL RUTHERFORD

**From the fullness of his grace, we have
all received one blessing after another.**
John 1:16

FOR THE CLASS OF 2008

The golden rule for understanding in spiritual matters is not intellect, but obedience.
—OSWALD CHAMBERS

Here's how we can be sure that we know God in the right way: Keep his commandments.

1 John 2:3 MSG

FOR THE CLASS OF 2008

The trouble with our times is that the
future is not what it used to be.
—PAUL VALÉRY

We fix our eyes not on what is seen,
but on what is unseen. For what is seen
is temporary, but what is unseen is
eternal.

2 Corinthians 4:18

FOR THE CLASS OF 2008

No man need stay the way he is.
—HARRY EMERSON FOSDICK

The night is far spent, the day is at hand. Therefore let us cast off the works of darkness, and let us put on the armor of light.

Romans 13:12 NKJV

FOR THE CLASS OF 2008

A ship in harbor is safe, but that is
not what ships are built for.
—WILLIAM SHEDD

**You are the world's light—a city on a
hill, glowing in the night for all to see.
Don't hide your light!**

Matthew 5:14-15 TLB

FOR THE CLASS OF 2008

Living in the moment brings you a sense
of reverence for all of life's blessings.
—OPRAH WINFREY

**So don't be anxious about tomorrow.
God will take care of your tomorrow
too. Live one day at a time.**

Matthew 6:34 TLB

FOR THE CLASS OF 2008

GOD'S LITTLE INSTRUCTION BOOK

Wisdom is the combination of honesty and
knowledge applied through experience.
—DENIS WAITLEY

**Teach us to number our days aright,
that we may gain a heart of wisdom.**
Psalm 90:12

FOR THE CLASS OF 2008

God does not love us because we are valuable.
We are valuable because God loves us.
—Archbishop Fulton J. Sheen

**The Lord delights in those who fear
him, who put their hope in his
unfailing love.**

Psalm 147:11

FOR THE CLASS OF 2008

The world is governed more by
appearances than realities.
—DANIEL WEBSTER

**These are a shadow of the things that
were to come; the reality, however, is
found in Christ.**

Colossians 2:17

FOR THE CLASS OF 2008

You can tell the character of every man
when you see how he receives praise.
—SENECA

**God resists the proud, but gives grace
to the humble.**

James 4:6 NKJV

FOR THE CLASS OF 2008

The goal of life is to find out God's will and to do it.
—MARIA VON TRAPP

Just tell me what to do and I will do it, Lord. As long as I live I'll wholeheartedly obey.

Psalm 119:33-34 TLB

Life can only be understood backwards;
but it must be lived forwards.
—SØREN KIERKEGAARD

This is what the LORD says—your
Redeemer, the Holy One of Israel: "I
am the LORD your God, who teaches
you what is best for you, who directs
you in the way you should go."

Isaiah 48:17

FOR THE CLASS OF 2008

It is better to have a permanent income
than to be fascinating.
—OSCAR WILDE

**Lazy hands make a man poor, but
diligent hands bring wealth.**

Proverbs 10:4

FOR THE CLASS OF 2008

To be a Christian means to forgive
the inexcusable, because God has
forgiven the inexcusable in you.
—C. S. LEWIS

Bear with each other and forgive
whatever grievances you may have
against one another. Forgive as the
Lord forgave you.

Colossians 3:13

FOR THE CLASS OF 2008

How wonderful it is that nobody need wait a single moment before starting to improve the world.
—ANNE FRANK

As we have opportunity, let us do good to all people.

Galatians 6:10

FOR THE CLASS OF 2008

The Scriptures were not given to increase our
knowledge but to change our lives.
—D. L. MOODY

**Show me your ways, O LORD, teach me
your paths.**

Psalm 25:4

FOR THE CLASS OF 2008

Don't allow the future to scare you.
—TENNESSEE WILLIAMS

Whoever trusts in the LORD is kept safe.

Proverbs 29:25

FOR THE CLASS OF 2008

Great men are little men expanded; great
lives are ordinary lives intensified.
—WILFRED A. PETERSON

**Those who have served well gain an
excellent standing and great assurance
in their faith in Christ Jesus.**

1 Timothy 3:13

FOR THE CLASS OF 2008

The greater part of our happiness or misery depends
on our disposition and not our circumstances.
—Martha Washington

I know how to live on almost nothing
or with everything. I have learned the
secret of contentment in every
situation.

Philippians 4:12 TLB

FOR THE CLASS OF 2008

Give light, and the darkness will disappear of itself.
—DESIDERIUS ERASMUS

God saw that the light was good, and He separated the light from the darkness.

Genesis 1:4

FOR THE CLASS OF 2008

Take time to deliberate; but when the time for action arrives, stop thinking and go on.
—ANDREW JACKSON

Rise up; this matter is in your hands. We will support you, so take courage and do it.

Ezra 10:4

FOR THE CLASS OF 2008

Do not borrow trouble by dreading
tomorrow. It is the dark menace of the future
that makes cowards of us all.
—Dorothy Dix

**He will command his angels
concerning you to guard you in all your
ways.**

Psalm 91:11

FOR THE CLASS OF 2008

Who lives in fear will never be a free man.
—HORACE

The LORD is with me; I will not be afraid.

Psalm 118:6

FOR THE CLASS OF 2008

Faith is not belief without proof, but
trust without reservations.
—ELTON TRUEBLOOD

**As for God, His way is perfect; the
word of the LORD is proven; He is a
shield to all who trust in Him.**

Psalm 18:30 NKJV

FOR THE CLASS OF 2008

Lord, be pleased to shake my clay cottage
before Thou throwest it down.
—THOMAS FULLER

**So then each of us shall give account of
himself to God.**

Romans 14:12 NKJV

FOR THE CLASS OF 2008

To wisdom belongs the intellectual apprehension of things eternal; to knowledge, the rational apprehension of things temporal.

—St. Augustine

He who has knowledge spares his words.

Proverbs 17:27 NKJV

FOR THE CLASS OF 2008

To speak painful truth through loving
words, that is friendship.
—HENRY WARD BEECHER

Faithful are the wounds of a friend.
Proverbs 27:6 NKJV

FOR THE CLASS OF 2008

Let us not ask of the Lord deceitful riches, nor the good things of this world, nor transitory honors; but let us ask for light.

—SAINT GREGORY OF NAZIANZUS

Delight yourself also in the LORD, and He shall give you the desires of your heart.

Psalm 37:4 NKJV

FOR THE CLASS OF 2008

God's help is nearer than the door.
—Irish Proverb

I am with you and will watch over you wherever you go.

Genesis 28:15

FOR THE CLASS OF 2008

From the errors of others, a wise
man corrects his own.
—Publilius Syrus

**Those who are wise will shine like the
brightness of the heavens.**

Daniel 12:3

FOR THE CLASS OF 2008

Thoughts lead on to purposes; purposes go forth in action; actions form habits; habits decide character; and character fixes our destiny.

—TYRON EDWARDS

The purposes of a man's heart are deep waters, but a man of understanding draws them out.

Proverbs 20:5

FOR THE CLASS OF 2008

Without prayer, we return to our own
ability rather than to God.
—BETH MOORE

**I am glad to boast about how weak I
am; I am glad to be a living
demonstration of Christ's power,
instead of showing off my own power
and abilities.**

2 Corinthians 12:9 TLB

FOR THE CLASS OF 2008

God dwells in eternity, but time dwells
in God. He has already lived all our
tomorrows as he has lived all our yesterdays.
—A. W. TOZER

**Surely I am with you always, to the
very end of the age.**

Matthew 28:20

FOR THE CLASS OF 2008

If thou desire the love of God and man, be humble; for the proud heart, as it loves none but itself, so it is beloved of none but itself.

—FRANCES QUARLES

Do not think of yourself more highly than you ought.

Romans 12:3

FOR THE CLASS OF 2008

Let your words be the genuine picture of your heart.
—JOHN WESLEY

My mouth shall speak wisdom, and the meditation of my heart shall give understanding.

Psalm 49:3 NKJV

FOR THE CLASS OF 2008

Let there be kindness in your face, in your eyes, in your smile, in the warmth of your greeting.... Don't only give your care, but give your heart as well.
—MOTHER TERESA

Do not forget to do good and to share with others, for with such sacrifices God is pleased.

Hebrews 13:16

FOR THE CLASS OF 2008

In the Kingdom of God, service is not a stepping-stone to nobility: it is nobility, the only kind of nobility that is recognized.
—T. W. MANSON

Serve wholeheartedly, as if you were serving the Lord, not men.

Ephesians 6:7

FOR THE CLASS OF 2008

I shall tell you a great secret, my friend. Do not wait for the last judgment, it takes place every day.
—ALBERT CAMUS

You also must be ready, because the Son of Man will come at an hour when you do not expect him.

Luke 12:40

FOR THE CLASS OF 2008

Every man is a missionary, now and forever, for good
or for evil, whether he intends or designs it or not.
—THOMAS CHALMERS

**I have set before you life and death,
blessing and cursing; therefore choose
life, that both you and your
descendants may live.**

Deuteronomy 30:19 NKJV

FOR THE CLASS OF 2008

It often happens that those of whom we speak
least on earth are best known in heaven.
—Nicholas Caussin

**You are a chosen people, a royal
priesthood, a holy nation, a people
belonging to God, that you may declare
the praises of him who called you out
of darkness into his wonderful light.**

1 Peter 2:9

FOR THE CLASS OF 2008

Is it not wonderful news to believe that
salvation lies outside ourselves?
—MARTIN LUTHER

**If from there you seek the LORD your
God, you will find him if you look for
him with all your heart and with all
your soul.**

Deuteronomy 4:29

FOR THE CLASS OF 2008

Man's life is of God, not of his goods,
however abundant they may be.
—HENRY ALFORD

No one can serve two masters. Either he will hate the one and love the other, or he will be devoted to the one and despise the other. You cannot serve both God and Money.

Matthew 6:24

FOR THE CLASS OF 2008

Snuggle in God's arms. When you are hurting, when you feel lonely, left out, let Him cradle you, comfort you, reassure you of His all-sufficient power and love.

—KAY ARTHUR

Staying right at the center of God's love, keeping your arms open and outstretched, ready for the mercy of our Master, Jesus Christ. This is the unending life, the real life!

Jude 1:21 MSG

FOR THE CLASS OF 2008

I am an old man and have known a great many troubles, but most of them never happened.
—MARK TWAIN

I will lie down and sleep in peace, for you alone, O LORD, make me dwell in safety.

Psalm 4:8

FOR THE CLASS OF 2008

Happiness depends on what happens; joy does not.
—OSWALD CHAMBERS

**You have made known to me the path
of life; you will fill me with joy in your
presence, with eternal pleasures at
your right hand.**

Psalm 16:11

FOR THE CLASS OF 2008

Look upon your chastening as God's chariots sent to carry your soul into the high places of spiritual achievement.
—HANNAH WHITALL SMITH

As many as I love, I rebuke and chasten. Therefore be zealous and repent.

Revelation 3:19 NKJV

FOR THE CLASS OF 2008

God made the world round, so we would never
be able to see too far down the road.
—ISAK DINESEN

"For I know the plans I have for you,"
declares the LORD, "plans to prosper
you and not to harm you, plans to give
you hope and a future."

Jeremiah 29:11

FOR THE CLASS OF 2008

The most revolutionary statement in history is "Love Thy Enemy."
—ELDRIDGE CLEAVER

This is love: not that we loved God, but that he loved us and sent his Son as an atoning sacrifice for our sins.

1 John 4:10

FOR THE CLASS OF 2008

GOD'S LITTLE INSTRUCTION BOOK

Peace is not an absence of war; it is a virtue,
a state of mind, a disposition for
benevolence, confidence, justice.
—BARUCH SPINOZA

Seek peace and pursue it.

Psalm 34:14

FOR THE CLASS OF 2008

Thanksgiving is the language of heaven, and
we had better start to learn it if we are not
to be mere dumb aliens there.

—A. J. GOSSIP

**For every creature of God is good, and
nothing is to be refused if it is received
with thanksgiving.**

1 Timothy 4:4 NKJV

FOR THE CLASS OF 2008

Within your heart keep one still, secret
spot where dreams may go and, sheltered
so, may thrive and grow.
—LOUISE DRISCOLL

**Above all else, guard your heart, for it
is the wellspring of life.**

Proverbs 4:23

FOR THE CLASS OF 2008

God's investment in us is so great he
could not possibly abandon us.
—ERWIN W. LUTZER

**The LORD appeared to us in the past,
saying: "I have loved you with an
everlasting love; I have drawn you with
loving-kindness."**

Jeremiah 31:3

FOR THE CLASS OF 2008

We get one story, you and I, and one story alone.
God has established the elements, the setting, and
the climax and the resolution. It would be
a crime not to venture out, wouldn't it?
—DONALD MILLER

Whether you turn to the right or to the left, your ears will hear a voice behind you, saying, "This is the way; walk in it."

Isaiah 30:21

FOR THE CLASS OF 2008

God is not a deceiver, that He should offer to support us, and then, when we lean upon Him, should slip away from us.

—St. Augustine

Guard my life, for I am devoted to you. You are my God; save your servant who trusts in you.

Psalm 86:2

FOR THE CLASS OF 2008

Missions is less about the transportation of God from one place to another and more about the identification of a God who is already there.
—ROB BELL

And whatever you do, whether in word or deed, do it all in the name of the Lord Jesus, giving thanks to God the Father through him.

Colossians 3:17

FOR THE CLASS OF 2008

We can believe what we choose. We are answerable
for what we choose to believe.
—JOHN HENRY NEWMAN

**But without faith it is impossible to
please Him, for he who comes to God
must believe that He is, and that He is
a rewarder of those who diligently seek
Him.**

Hebrews 11:6 NKJV

FOR THE CLASS OF 2008

God does not give us everything we want, but
He does fulfill His promises ... leading us
along the best and straightest paths to Himself.

—DIETRICH BONHOEFFER

**In everything you do, put God first,
and he will direct you and crown your
efforts with success.**

Proverbs 3:6 TLB

FOR THE CLASS OF 2008

Fear defeats more people than any
other one thing in the world.
—Ralph Waldo Emerson

Perfect love drives out fear.

1 John 4:18

FOR THE CLASS OF 2008

If I find in myself a desire which no experience in this world can satisfy, the most probable explanation is that I was made for another world.

—C. S. LEWIS

You're no longer wandering exiles. This kingdom of faith is now your home country. You're no longer strangers or outsiders. You belong here, with as much right to the name Christian as anyone.

Ephesians 2:19 MSG

FOR THE CLASS OF 2008

Never fear shadows. They simply mean there's light shining somewhere nearby.
—RUTH E. RENKEL

Yea, though I walk through the valley of the shadow of death, I will fear no evil; for You are with me; Your rod and Your staff, they comfort me.

Psalm 23:4 NKJV

FOR THE CLASS OF 2008

Your worst days are never so bad that you are beyond the reach of God's grace. And your best days are never so good that you are beyond the need of God's grace.
—JERRY BRIDGES

God can pour on the blessings in astonishing ways so that you're ready for anything and everything, more than just ready to do what needs to be done.
2 Corinthians 9:8 MSG

FOR THE CLASS OF 2008

My faith isn't in the idea that I'm more moral than anybody else. My faith is in the idea that God and His love are greater than whatever sins any of us commit.
—RICH MULLINS

I sought the LORD, and he answered me; he delivered me from all my fears.
Psalm 34:4

FOR THE CLASS OF 2008

Pray for just enough illumination for the next step,
and then the courage to take it.
—DAVID CROWDER

**Be joyful in hope, patient in affliction,
faithful in prayer.**

Romans 12:12

FOR THE CLASS OF 2008

He loved me 'ere I knew him; and all my love
is due him; he plunged me to victory
beneath the cleansing flood.

—EUGENE M. BARTLETT

**Thanks be to God! He gives us the
victory through our Lord Jesus Christ.**

1 Corinthians 15:57

FOR THE CLASS OF 2008

GOD'S LITTLE INSTRUCTION BOOK

Theology is just what you really think about God, and if you're going to do that, you'd better use your mind and not just let it be a receptacle, a catch-all for whatever beliefs happen to be passing by.
—DALLAS WILLARD

For the word of God is living and active. Sharper than any double-edged sword, it penetrates even to dividing soul and spirit, joints and marrow; it judges the thoughts and attitudes of the heart.

Hebrews 4:12

FOR THE CLASS OF 2008

Any definition of a successful life
must include serving others.
—GEORGE H. W. BUSH

**He who is greatest among you shall be
your servant.**

Matthew 23:11 NKJV

FOR THE CLASS OF 2008

God never put anyone in a place too small to grow in.
—HENRIETTA MEARS

Give thanks in all circumstances, for this is God's will for you in Christ Jesus.

1 Thessalonians 5:18

FOR THE CLASS OF 2008

Act boldly and unseen forces will come to your aid.
—Dorothea Brande

We have the Lord our God to fight our battles for us!

2 Chronicles 32:8 TLB

FOR THE CLASS OF 2008

Not only do we not know God except through Jesus Christ; We do not even know ourselves except through Jesus Christ.
—BLAISE PASCAL

Cheerfully pleasing God is the main thing, and that's what we aim to do, regardless of our conditions.

2 Corinthians 5:9 MSG

FOR THE CLASS OF 2008

Pray often, for prayer is a shield to the soul, a sacrifice to God, and a scourge for Satan.
—JOHN BUNYAN

The prayer of a righteous man is powerful and effective.

James 5:16

FOR THE CLASS OF 2008

The essence of temptation is the invitation
to live independently of God.
—NEIL ANDERSON

**I am the vine; you are the branches. If
a man remains in me and I in him, he
will bear much fruit; apart from me
you can do nothing.**

John 15:5

FOR THE CLASS OF 2008

To be of a peaceable spirit brings peace along with it.
— THOMAS WATSON

Are you tired? Worn out? Burned out on religion? Come to me. Get away with me and you'll recover your life. I'll show you how to take a real rest. Walk with me and work with me— watch how I do it. Learn the unforced rhythms of grace.

Matthew 11:28 MSG

FOR THE CLASS OF 2008

Learn the luxury of doing good.
—Oliver Goldsmith

Do not withhold good from those who deserve it, when it is in your power to act.

Proverbs 3:27

FOR THE CLASS OF 2008

Sainthood lies in the habit of referring
the smallest actions to God.
—C. S. LEWIS

Praise Him for His mighty acts; praise Him according to His excellent greatness!

Psalm 150:2 NKJV

FOR THE CLASS OF 2008

Truth, like surgery, may hurt but it cures.
—HAN SUYIN

Speaking the truth in love, we will in all things grow up into him who is the Head, that is, Christ.

Ephesians 4:15

FOR THE CLASS OF 2008

The capacity to care is the thing which gives life its deepest significance.

—PABLO CASALS

Carry each other's burdens, and in this way you will fulfill the law of Christ.

Galatians 6:2

FOR THE CLASS OF 2008

The Bible knows nothing of solitary religion.
—JOHN WESLEY

You can develop a healthy, robust community that lives right with God and enjoy its results only if you do the hard work of getting along with each other, treating each other with dignity and honor.

James 3:18 MSG

FOR THE CLASS OF 2008

No sacrifice can be too great to make for Him who gave His life for me.
—CHARLES STUDD

Christ's love compels us, because we are convinced that one died for all.
2 Corinthians 5:14

FOR THE CLASS OF 2008

And as you learn how to die, you start losing all your illusions, and you start being capable now of true intimacy and love.

—EUGENE H. PETERSON

For if you live according to the sinful nature, you will die; but if by the Spirit you put to death the misdeeds of the body, you will live.

Romans 8:13

FOR THE CLASS OF 2008

My extreme preoccupation with knowing God's will for me may only indicate, contrary to what is often thought, that I am overconcerned with myself, not a Christlike interest in the well-being of others or in the glory of God.

—DALLAS WILLARD

The mind controlled by the Spirit is life and peace.

Romans 8:6

FOR THE CLASS OF 2008

Obedience to the call of Christ nearly always costs everything to two people: the one who is called, and the one who loves that one.
—OSWALD CHAMBERS

If you will indeed obey My voice and keep My covenant, then you shall be a special treasure to Me above all people; for all the earth is Mine.

Exodus 19:5 NKJV

FOR THE CLASS OF 2008

What we are is God's gift to us. What we become is our gift to God.
—Eleanor Powell

Every good and perfect gift is from above, coming down from the Father of the heavenly lights.

James 1:17

FOR THE CLASS OF 2008

You can give without loving, but you cannot love without giving.
—AMY CARMICHAEL

It is more blessed to give than to receive.

Acts 20:35

FOR THE CLASS OF 2008

Call on God, but row away from the rocks.
—HUNTER S. THOMPSON

Wisdom and good judgment live together, for wisdom knows where to discover knowledge and understanding.

Proverbs 8:12 TLB

FOR THE CLASS OF 2008

You are saved—seek to be like your Savior.
—CHARLES SPURGEON

I want to know Christ and the power
of his resurrection and the fellowship
of sharing in his sufferings, becoming
like him in his death.

Philippians 3:10

FOR THE CLASS OF 2008

Though our feelings come and go,
God's love for us does not.
—C. S. LEWIS

**Great is his faithfulness; his
lovingkindness begins afresh each day.**
Lamentations 3:23 TLB

FOR THE CLASS OF 2008

There is nothing that we can see on earth which does not either show the wretchedness of man or the mercy of God. One either sees the powerlessness of man without God, or the strength of man with God.

—Blaise Pascal

Take up your positions; stand firm and see the deliverance the Lord will give you.

2 Chronicles 20:17

FOR THE CLASS OF 2008

Success consists of getting up just
one more time than you fall.
—OLIVER GOLDSMITH

**I can do everything through him who
gives me strength.**

Philippians 4:13

FOR THE CLASS OF 2008

I am convinced that faith sometimes means knowing God can whether or not he does.
—BETH MOORE

If we are thrown into the blazing furnace, the God we serve is able to save us from it.... But even if he does not, we want you to know, O king, that we will not serve your gods.

Daniel 3:17-18

FOR THE CLASS OF 2008

The stars are constantly shining, but often we
do not see them until the dark hours.
—EARL RINEY

**My help comes from the LORD, the
Maker of heaven and earth.**

Psalm 121:2

FOR THE CLASS OF 2008

A fault, once denied, is twice committed.
—FRENCH PROVERB

**Search me, O God, and know my heart;
test my thoughts. Point out anything
you find in me that makes you sad.**
Psalms 139:23-24 TLB

FOR THE CLASS OF 2008

I have decided to stick with love. Hate is too great a burden to bear.
—MARTIN LUTHER KING JR.

Do everything in love.

1 Corinthians 16:14

FOR THE CLASS OF 2008

At the height of laughter, the universe is flung
into a kaleidoscope of new possibilities.
—JEAN HOUSTON

**He will yet fill your mouth with
laughter and your lips with shouts of
joy.**

Job 8:21

FOR THE CLASS OF 2008

Few things are impossible to diligence
and skill. Great works are performed,
not by strength, but perseverance.
—SAMUEL JOHNSON

**We want each of you to show this same
diligence to the very end, in order to
make your hope sure.**

Hebrews 6:11

FOR THE CLASS OF 2008

Learn from yesterday; live for today;
hope for tomorrow.
—ALBERT EINSTEIN

**We have this hope as an anchor for the
soul, firm and secure.**

Hebrews 6:19

FOR THE CLASS OF 2008

Only one thing has to change for us to know
happiness in our lives: where we focus our attention.
—GREG ANDERSON

**Jesus said, "'Love the Lord your God
with all your passion and prayer and
intelligence.'"**

Matthew 22:37 MSG

FOR THE CLASS OF 2008

Four things for success: Work and
pray, think and believe.
—NORMAN VINCENT PEALE

**She opens her arms to the poor and
extends her hands to the needy.**

Proverbs 31:20

FOR THE CLASS OF 2008

Beware that you do not lose the substance
by grasping at the shadow.
—AESOP

Give your servant a discerning heart.
1 Kings 3:9

FOR THE CLASS OF 2008

He who accepts evil without protesting
against it is really cooperating with it.
—MARTIN LUTHER KING JR.

I will have nothing to do with evil.
                                    Psalm 101:4

FOR THE CLASS OF 2008

Never be afraid to trust an unknown
future to a known God.
—CORRIE TEN BOOM

**I will turn the darkness into light
before them and make the rough places
smooth.**

Isaiah 42:16

FOR THE CLASS OF 2008

I decided to leave my home and become a nun, and since then I've never doubted that I've done the right thing. It was the will of God. It was His choice.

—MOTHER TERESA

Your ears shall hear a word behind you, saying, "This is the way, walk in it," whenever you turn to the right hand or whenever you turn to the left.

Isaiah 30:21 NKJV

FOR THE CLASS OF 2008

Where fear is present, wisdom cannot be.
—LACTANTIUS

The LORD is my light and my salvation—whom shall I fear?

Psalm 27:1

FOR THE CLASS OF 2008

To see a world in a grain of sand and a heaven in a wild flower, hold infinity in the palm of your hand and eternity in an hour.

—WILLIAM BLAKE

[God] has not left himself without testimony: He has shown kindness by giving you rain from heaven and crops in their seasons.

Acts 14:17

FOR THE CLASS OF 2008

When I despair, I remember that all through history,
the way of truth and love has always won.
—MAHATMA GANDHI

**The Lord knows how to rescue godly
men from trials.**

2 Peter 2:9

FOR THE CLASS OF 2008

A Christian is someone who shares the
sufferings of God in the world.
—DIETRICH BONHOEFFER

**Consider it pure joy, my brothers,
whenever you face trials of many
kinds, because you know that the
testing of your faith develops
perseverance.**

James 1:2-3

FOR THE CLASS OF 2008

Always seek peace between your heart and God,
but in this world, always be careful to remain
ever-restless, never satisfied, and always
abounding in the work of the Lord.
—Jim Elliot

**In everything set them an example by
doing what is good.**

Titus 2:7

FOR THE CLASS OF 2008

I went on with my eager pursuit after more holiness and conformity to Christ. The heaven I desired was a heaven of holiness.

—JONATHAN EDWARDS

The heavens declare the glory of God; the skies proclaim the work of his hands.

Psalm 19:1

FOR THE CLASS OF 2008

Avoiding danger is no safer in the long
run than outright exposure. Life is either
a daring adventure, or nothing.
—Helen Keller

**Alive, I'm Christ's messenger; dead, I'm
his bounty. Life versus even more life! I
can't lose.**

Philippians 1:21 MSG

FOR THE CLASS OF 2008

Every action of our lives touches on some chord that will vibrate in eternity.
—EDWIN HUBBEL CHAPIN

In the same way, let your light shine before men, that they may see your good deeds and praise your Father in heaven.

Matthew 5:16

FOR THE CLASS OF 2008

Faith never knows where it is being led, but it loves and knows the One who is leading.
—OSWALD CHAMBERS

We live by faith, not by sight.
2 Corinthians 5:7

FOR THE CLASS OF 2008

Leap, and the net will appear.
—JOHN BURROUGHS

As for God, His way is perfect; the word of the LORD is proven; He is a shield to all who trust in Him.

2 Samuel 22:31 NKJV

FOR THE CLASS OF 2008

What God does, he does well.
—Paul Tillich

I praise you because I am fearfully and wonderfully made; your works are wonderful.

Psalm 139:14

FOR THE CLASS OF 2008

For it is in giving that we receive;
It is in pardoning that we are pardoned;
It is in dying that we are born to eternal life.
—St. Francis of Assisi

**Even I, the Messiah, am not here to be
served, but to help others, and to give
my life as a ransom for many.**

Mark 10:45 TLB

FOR THE CLASS OF 2008

Rare as is true love, true friendship is still rarer.
—JEAN DE LA FONTAINE

I have called you friends, for everything that I learned from my Father I have made known to you.

John 15:15

FOR THE CLASS OF 2008

Character is doing the right thing when nobody's looking. There are too many people who think that the only thing that's right is to get by, and the only thing that's wrong is to get caught.

—J. C. WATTS

There is a way that seems right to a man, but in the end it leads to death.

Proverbs 14:12

FOR THE CLASS OF 2008

Believe in something larger than yourself.
—BARBARA BUSH

Now faith is the substance of things hoped for, the evidence of things not seen.

Hebrews 11:1 NKJV

FOR THE CLASS OF 2008

Honesty is the first chapter of the book of wisdom.
—THOMAS JEFFERSON

**You deserve honesty from the heart;
yes, utter sincerity and truthfulness.
Oh, give me this wisdom.**

Psalm 51:6 TLB

FOR THE CLASS OF 2008

What the caterpillar calls the end of the world,
the Master calls a butterfly.
—RICHARD BACH

We, who with unveiled faces all reflect the Lord's glory, are being transformed into his likeness with ever-increasing glory.

2 Corinthians 3:18

FOR THE CLASS OF 2008